EXPLORING
THE POWER
OF YOUR
POTENTIALS

InterMedia Productionz

EXPLORING THE POWER OF YOUR POTENTIALS

e-book ISBN: 978-978-650-4
Print ISBN: 978-978-977-651-1

Designed and Published by:
InterMedia Productionz
+234 (0) 706 383 9255

DEDICATION

This book is dedicated to all my protégées and other young people who have come into my life – past and present. Your desire to find your purpose in God led me into the search of these truths I have written in the pages of this book.

This book is in attempt to document some answers to the questions you have asked, and I hope you find understanding by the help of the Holy Spirit and also are equipped with scriptural principles to help as many others you come across in your journey of eternal relevance.

Love y'all.

ACKNOWLEDGEMENT

My sincere appreciation goes to Coach George Unogu, founder, Plarta Consulting, for your mentorship and fatherly counsel that has guided me through the process of publishing this book.

Every moment spent with you inspires me on how to realize my set goals. Serving your grace has been more than just a privilege to me. I just want to say a big THANK YOU for being there for me.

Pastor (Mrs.) Eno Unogu, a mother in Zion, whose strides and wisdom inspire me so much, thank you for being such a huge blessing to me.

Pastor Suoton Elihai, a mother with a heart of gold. You picked me and brought me in as a stranger. You took your chances on me and even through the rough times, you have shown your love is deeper than words can say. Thank you Ma.

To my mother, the great womb that bore me and have never stopped nurturing the seed of God in my life, Mrs. Evelyn Abiama, words would fail me to express to the world what your love and tireless intercession means to me. This world will honour you and call you blessed among other women.

To my second mum Mrs. Priye, and her adorable husband Mr. Lekan Akinyoyenu, where do I start to tell of your close touch? In most cases, you have been the first to respond in words of encouragement and finances when this vision needs such. My story cannot be written without you, and so the blessings of this global impact will not elude you, in Jesus' name. Amen!

To every other member of my family and close friends, who see to it that I remain motivated to deliver this divine mandate, I appreciate you all. You mean the world to me.

God bless you all.

FOREWORD

Just like pregnancy, I feel the burden to help you fulfill God's purpose for your life. It's about time you stopped living your life by default setting. Be intentional about living a more fulfilling life, for it is in the premise of your purpose you can find true fulfilment.

In spite of your fears, deficiencies, failures, successes or achievements so far, I dare to tell you, there's a whole lot more within you than you are aware of.

Where a farmer cannot grow crops, he calls the land barren until a miner discovers mineral deposits therein, then the barren land becomes a valued property attracting expatriates and sophisticated machinery. Don't let anybody or circumstance tag you barren. You are still in the discovery process and this book will guide you through this process till you unveil your eternal relevance.

Minerals are substances that are naturally potent in the earth, which are not products of any animal or vegetable matter. That's too deep for a farmer to relate with. So if thus far, you have been dealing with 'farmers', there is a tendency you have been under-explored, under-productive and undervalued.

This book in your hand is going to uncover the underlying treasure you are made of and further guide you into ways you can explore new possibilities you never knew you were capable of.

This book is a Word-based destiny guide for young people and others who want to discover purpose on a deeper level.

-Chris-Eden

TABLE OF CONTENT

INTRODUCTION

It is interesting to explore the concept of potential, as it is a major concern for everybody that has ever desired to do anything worthwhile. Potential is concerned with the prospective outcome of an event, untapped quality that can be developed into something of value by which needs may be met and gain made.

My concern therefore, is to have you examine yourself in the light of the divine deposits God has made inside of you and engage all your might in the value-adding process required to make you a phenomenon to be reckoned with in your lifetime.

This book avails you with in-depth workable steps on how to tap within and release your desired future. With such a practical approach, I trust the Holy Spirit to guide your thoughts into destiny unfolding ideas. So my objective in writing this book is to help you observe to do, all you must do, about all you can do to become all you can be. You must understand this: you can know all you know, but until action is taken in the direction of what you know, nothing is done.

"This Book of the Law shall not depart from your mouth, but you shall meditate in it day and night, that you may OBSERVE TO DO according to all that is written in it. For then you will make your way prosperous, and then you will have good success." Josh. 1:8.

You don't just observe to know, but to do. Your success is in your doing.

01: IT'S IN YOU... YES YOU_

"But we have this treasure in earthen vessels that the excellence (superiority, distinction, value) of the power may be of God and not of us." -2Cor. 4:7

Observe the scripture clearly states "we have this treasure in earthen vessels...." It doesn't say we will have.... It is not a promise neither is it a prayer point. We don't pray to have it. This means everybody already has this treasure...divine deposits... potentials.

It goes further to say that the quality, the excellence, the value of your potential... what makes it unique is of God, in the sense that you don't have it because you worked for it. You did not labour to have it.

It is not measured or requited to anyone based on any academic, social or spiritual standing. It then means you can't do anything to improve or deplete it.

The omnipotent God has shared a bit of His potency with every single human being... you inclusive. This is the treasure in earthen vessels, so that these inbuilt abilities may be credited to God the creator only, as the origin. Until you see yourself the way God sees you, how you see God makes no difference. God says the treasure is in you. Believe it!

Talking about potential, we will not be able to explore this concept until we consider 'PURPOSE', because potential is a factor of purpose.

PURPOSE:

Your purpose is God's original intention for your creation. It is your essence for living. It is the reason you were born.

These are words we have heard over and over again but many of us don't seem to understand it. That is why people crave and chase after frivolities to satisfy their internal desire for fulfilment.

Permit me to say here that nothing you chase now is as important as living out what God created you for. That is why time after time you seem to have achieved a big goal that was your greatest target, yet shortly after, you lose fulfilment. Even if you have all your cravings now, if you are outside your purpose you will never be fulfilled. But see a man who may not even have a good shelter over his head, and is walking in the purpose of God for his life, he exudes that aura of fulfilment.

However, it is not possible to walk in your purpose and not enjoy the provisions thereof. The purposes of God are always perfect. When you clock in on it, every other thing is attracted to you.

"And God is able to make all grace abound toward you, that you, always having all sufficiency in all things, may have an abundance for every good work." 2Cor.9:8.

Everybody was born to be a star, but your star will never be noticed until you find purpose. The discovery of purpose unveils the star in you. Watch this:

"...For this purpose the Son of God was manifested,..." 1John 3:8.

Hold on for a moment! Did you observe something there? Purpose precedes manifestation. You cannot manifest without purpose. You may live and die in obscurity, despite your gifts and great ideas, if you don't discover your purpose.

What is your pursuit right now? If it is outside the purpose of God you will never be fulfilled. Your purpose in life is the reason why God created you. It is the Divine motive behind your creation. So why should you be here on earth doing every other thing without fulfilling the motive of God for your life? "If you're alive there's a purpose for your life." (Rick Warren).

Whatever you do now, if it is not purpose oriented, you can only derive temporary satisfaction and superficial excitement from it, but not fulfilment. Because it is only in the premise of God's purpose for your life you can find true fulfilment. "Efforts and courage are not enough without purpose and direction." (John F. Kennedy). Fulfilment is the product of desire aligned with purpose. Find your purpose.

PURPOSE ACCESSORIES

Purpose always come with packages of abilities, fancies, inclinations, respective areas of special interest, skills, talents intuitions, instincts, perspectives, perception.... these are certain bundles that come with purpose.

You ask yourself how come Ben is able to do certain things seamlessly and Jack, equally masculine, is not able to do that. How come Cynthia is interested in one thing and Audrey who is just another girl like her, has no flair is that area? "If you can't figure out your purpose, figure out your passion. For your passion will lead you right into your purpose." (Bishop T.D. Jakes)

I was branding for a roofing company some time back and in one of my meetings with the manager, we had some extra-curricular discussions about 'individual uniqueness'. I picked up a brochure from his table and observed some colour-grading errors and pointed it out to him. Notice when I stepped into the office, I didn't really care how the office looks. I have no flair for that. Meanwhile, there are some people when they step into a place like that, their eyes would catch one area that is not properly arranged, a window blind that is out of place or a wall decoration that would be better off somewhere else.

 Ask yourself , what is your flair? (Use the Activity Sheet)

I stepped into my neighbor's house to get some movie CDs to relax with, after a very busy work week, but guess what? I left there with messages of men of God I admire.

I ask again, what is your flair? There are certain preachers I won't even naturally listen to, though they preach the Word of God. Why is that? I am inclined by purpose to certain areas of interest which is unique to me.

My purpose comes with these packages, they are inbuilt. It took me some time to discover my flair and anybody going through the pages of this book can follow these steps and do same. "The meaning of life is to find your gift. The purpose of life is to give it away." (Pablo Picasso).

WHAT'S YOUR FLAIR?

Is it not interesting how everybody hears a sound from the speakers, but you hear a distortion in the sound that makes you uncomfortable and disoriented for the rest of the session, figuring out what could possibly be the cause and solution to a problem nobody else even observes? That is an indication you may have an inclination towards sound engineering or something related to that.

What is you flair? How come you see things others don't notice? Have you ever wondered why you do things the way you do them? How come you are so different from other people in your perspective and opinions?

I came to realize that your purpose is the identity difference between you and everyone else. Even if you were born a twin, you may not be differentiated by your appearance, except by your fingerprint, but your fingerprint is not a strong enough difference as compared to your purpose.

In the eyes of God, He is not looking at your fingerprint, but your purpose. There are some friends or family members that have being together for so long that they think such relationships are inseparable, but I bet purpose has a way of separating you.

The reason one person may have to reseat an exam that the other person, though less brilliant, would smash in one sitting, could just be Purpose. What God is preparing one for is different from what He is preparing the other for.

That you've failed at something, does not make you a failure in life. Be encouraged to know that every pain you've been through is to bring you to a defining moment when it would all make sense why you had to be the one to lose the job, be victimized, be betrayed, drop out of school, lose a loved one, or whatever it is. God is prepping you up for something bigger than how you feel or what you think is going on around you. These are all making up the narrative of your success story. All you have to do is trust God through the process. Follow me closely.

I want you to believe you are here for a reason and your purpose is greater than your pain.

BE INTENTIONAL

I have come to realized that it is extreme religious irresponsibility to think that God will bring your destiny to pass without you doing anything about it, just because He is the originator of it.

You may be called into ministry in any capacity; you've always known it by traces, dreams or confirmations from other people, but how come what you are presently involved with has no bearing with that assignment? Some are waiting for God to appear in the sky and magically put them on stage. It won't happen like that. It defies God's order of operation.

You cannot fulfill purpose by chance. You have to be intentional about your pursuit for the expression of your destiny. It involves you just as much as it involves God. Your destiny fulfilment is a partnership venture between God and you. God inspires your heart with an idea, you perspire to work it out. Don't be lazy about it.

If you ever believe God has made a deposit in you, this is a call-up to responsibility for your next outcome in life. You have to do something with it. The days of taking the backseat of your own life and letting other people or circumstances drive you into fate, are over. You have to believe in yourself well enough to step forward, face your fears. It's ok to move against the tide, counter the trend, and make an indelible mark of eternal relevance. I'd rather die fighting an enemy outside, than to be defeated by self-doubt.

The scripture says, ***"Arise and shine ..."*** Isa. 60:1. You cannot manifest your destiny maintaining same old disposition you have. You have to engage in a conscious shift in your mind and any other area necessary. You may need to relocate somewhere else, enroll for some formal training, or change your line of business or course in school.

The truth is, to fulfill your purpose in life, you may experience some form of disorientation so as to reorder your life and priorities in the right direction.

I'm reminded of how my friends and I used to play street soccer, as kids. Sometimes, we peg sticks at both ends, which serve as the goal posts for each team, respectively. Your scores increase by the number of times you're able to strike the ball to hit the stick of your opponent. So we try so hard to play our way to an angle from whence we can take a shot at that stick. Lol! Yeah!

This is exactly how purpose is. It is just one spot on this field of life play. Everywhere else is missing the mark and would credit you with no score. This is the set point for your purpose. Everywhere else is a wrong place. Where purpose is not defined, you're shortchanged in your life endeavours.

What I'm sharing with you here is how to work it out. Don't die with such a great impact you never gave an expression because you were lazing about finding excuses for not doing much. I nudge you to stand up, take up your bed and do some moving. Take responsibility for your next move from here. God has programmed your next height as a function of your deliberate step off this comfort zone, so don't expect this to happen by miracle. If it would ever happen, it's up to you. You're a stock of great potentials waiting for exploration.

In closing, I leave you with this: In a chase between a lion and a deer, many times the deer wins. Because the lion runs for food, but the deer runs for life. Here's the lesson: Purpose is more important than need. Live for something more.

ACTIVITY SHEET

1. What do you have Flair for?
2. What are the Purpose Accessories you can identify in your life?

3. What steps can you take from now toward developing and expressing yourself?

02: **POTENTIAL_**

"But we have this treasure in earthen vessels that the excellence (superiority, distinction, value) of the power may be of God and not of us." -2Cor. 4:7

For the sake of this study, I'd like to consider what I call THE 3 P'S OF PURPOSE: *Potential, Process and Product*. These are the essential factors that make up Purpose. The fulfilment of every great destiny is tied to these 3P's.

POTENTIALS:

This is where Potential fits into the equation. It would have been improper to talk about potential without examining the framework on which it builds, which is Purpose.

Everyone was born with one special ability or another. It would be disapproving, quarrying or questioning the authenticity of God's creation to believe that you have none, or what you have is not good enough.

Liabilities are nothing but denied potentials. We are divine packs of great treasures. It is already in you. You're a complete package!

You see a little child failing in Maths and other subjects in school and the teacher's remark says the child is incapable of learning. Even at that, I dare you to believe that child already has in Him an inbuilt treasure.

Before Samson was born, the father questioned God to tell them the rule of his life (*See Judg. 13:12*). How many parents inquire of the Lord to know the divine program for their children? The children the Lord has given you are His heritage (*See Ps. 127:3*), and you think you don't need a blue print description from the Creator on how the child should be raised?

"There is no man living who isn't capable of doing more than he thinks he can do." (Henry Ford) There is something more you can do that you have not done yet. I don't care how people celebrate you now, there is something more you can do that you have not done yet.

Dear singer, there is a music you can compose that you have not composed yet. There is an idea you can develop that has not yet come forth. There is a project you can embark on that you have not tried out yet. There is a new design you can create but you have not done it yet.

There is a new horizon within you that you have not explored yet. These amount to uncultivated grounds within you.

You are wondering why you have the kind of harvest that does not match the needs in your life right now; you have a need of $1500 and you have just $600, you are broke. Now what God is saying is that, He has put as much grounds within you for you to cultivate and meet every need in your life and others around you, but how much results you have now depends on how much grounds you have cultivated. Harvest does not respond to needs known, but to seeds sown. Potentials are uncultivated grounds in your life. Common, let's get to work!

BREAK THAT POTENTIAL BOX

Too many cases running through my mind as I write this chapter: I know a man, a well-known photographer - at some point, he was the only photographer in the whole area where he lived, but he died without having a photo studio.

I know of another young man who was the best fine artist in our area back then. There was no match to the banners he used to make. I remember sitting to watch him creatively stencil shapes and letters for his work. But he just dropped all that skill at the invent of digital banners. But couldn't he have grown with the new trend, exploring his graphic ideas on a better pedestal? Just thinking!

I used to know some other young girls who were gifted in making beautiful flower vases, but just like the others cases, they aborted the process of their increasing proficiency because they never saw any much coming out of it, and so they dropped it to be counted among the unemployed youth.

I have also had my share of such failure. I began developing an inclination towards graphics over a decade ago and I started out doing little bits that turned out attracting so much admiration from people around, but just like those other cases, I never saw it as something I could undertake as a career someday.

I remember having an appointment with a big minister who had seen some of my designs and really desired to work with me for his next project. He asked me to see him in his office, and I went. He began by commending some of my designs he had seen and thereafter, threw a question at me, "What's your plan with this your talent; what do you intend doing with it?" Sincerely, hitherto, nobody had asked me that question, not even me asking myself. I was just enjoying my new found talent, but never sat to think it could amount to anything more.

Can you guess my response? Yeah! You must have guessed right. I told him I'm just passing time with it; I don't intend toeing that path for long. Once I said this, the man reclined on his seat and stared at me like he just wasted his time with a fool. I didn't understand any bit of that - the question he asked and now the staring. After a while, he said, "You can go now." Foolish me stood up, said "Thank you Sir", turned around and walked toward the door.

In that short distance to the door, I asked myself about a million times, "Is this all you really wanna do with this gift?" That was my first time of questioning myself about that, and it dawned on me that I really had no plan. I hadn't conceived any vision about the possibilities the future holds for me in this line.

I was sincere in my response to him, however, I was sincerely wrong. I was in error without knowing it. That is a mind limiting impediment called, Ignorance. It keeps you blinded to the possibility of greatness and thereby creates a habitat that sustains mediocrity around you. So you bask in your little circle for long, meanwhile, people you are better than are topping the chart and blazing new trails in that area.

"The leap from ignorance to wisdom is a question." (Dr. Mike Murdock) You are always a question away from ignorance and its consequences. That was me at that point, but I guess it was too late to recover that opportunity.

Shortly after that discussion, I heard that that minister invested some millions in setting up a printing press for another guy who later became the official producer of all their publications and publicity materials. Chaiii! That would have been me, but it's too late to cry over spilled milk.

That failure inspired me to get back and review my talent in the light of potential and further fine-tune my talent into a skill that is now one major stream of income for me.

Now I run a growing business with an expanding clientele within and outside Africa.

Potential is not anything you have done, but what you can do that you have not done yet. So when God looks at you

He sees Potential; not what you have done but what you are capable of doing based on His deposit in your life.

God is not interested in what you have done as much as what you can do. No matter who celebrates you now, your future is about what you can do that you have not done yet. So God spoke through Jeremiah to the men of Judah and Jerusalem *"...Break up you fallow grounds..."* Jer. 4:3. Break up your uncultivated grounds. Explore your potentials. You can do more than you have done so far. You can be bigger and better than you are right now.

It has been said that the greatest thinkers and inventors have only explored less than 10% of their mind capacity. Just imagine how it would be if you explore 100% of your potentials in your life time. Your imagination is your preview of future possibilities. Explore it!

Have you ever imagined that when God created the world He didn't create your phone, He didn't create the chair you are sitting on, He didn't create the houses you live in, He didn't create shoes neither did He create the kind of clothes you're wearing now. Anything that you are enjoying right now started as an idea a man like you sat down to process on how to explore what God has already potentiated in the universe, and engaged in discovering ways of bringing them out as tangible products for you to buy with your money. "Don't cheat the world of your contribution. Give it what you've got." (Steven Pressfield)

It always blows my mind when I think of how much I am making someone else rich by patronizing a product. The toothpaste you buy is somebody's idea. That's a potential that has been explored. Your potential can be of immense monetary value only when cultivated. Are you aware that some of the richest women in the world are producers of candies? They made it so available that you poor little earnings can afford it and they collect your money and remain richest people on earth.

Potential is a treasure box buried inside of you, waiting for you to break open. Don't die a celebrity that was never recognized. Don't die an imitation of someone else, meanwhile you were meant to be an original value that would have been duly rewarded. "There is no greater agony than bearing an untold story inside you." (Maya Angelou)

ACTIVITY SHEET

1. Can you remember anything you were good at or had serious interest in learning?
2. Why did you quit?
3. Which of them would you like to pick up again?

03: **PROCESSS**

"Most assuredly I say to you, unless a seed submits its potential to the soil and undergoes the process of insignificance, silence and despised, it never amounts to anything more; but if it dies, it eventually produces much harvest." (Paraphrased)" -John 12:24

Process is the developmental procedure involved in achieving anything. It is a set of actions to be taken in order to realize a possible outcome. Process is the bridge between ability and productivity. It is the bridge between what you can do and what you have done. It is the bridge between possibility and reality.

'Process' seems to be a strange word to the average 21st century youth. We live in a time when almost everything that was previously known to require some measure of sweat is now replaced with a quick-fix tech method. Today technology and the internet have made it so easy to do a whole lot in a short time.

Oh! I remember just when I was considering designing and production of greeting cards, mobile phone SMS ran that business aground. Now people just sit at home and draft lovely text messages and send just anywhere in the world and there won't be any need of taking the stress of going out to shop for a card and then posting it to the recipient. It is even a lot easier with the creation of other social media chat links.

Now it sounds like tales to the younger generation what it used to be back in the days. Most of them can't even fathom the manual system of posting and receiving letters and other valuables. I love the dynamism of this age, however, I still retain the deep lessons from the previous generation, because they teach a lot about process.

As a growing boy, I had shown interest in my father's photography business and at some point, proved myself capable of running my own and making some money for myself too. I think that became my foundation in media business eventually.

My dad armed me with an analogue camera along with the basic kit needed for photography. Back then, we used to have a roll of film fixed into the camera, with a limited number of exposures per roll. After exhausting a roll, you roll it back into the cartridge and take it to the lab for the process of printing that fine image captured.

When the cartridge goes to the lab, it comes out in a strap called Negative. The Negative presents that image with inverted colours – nothing traceable to the original beauty. It is from that negative the photographer selects the images to be printed and then returns to the lab for the final production of the beautiful pictures in its desired sizes.

I bet this is like a boring tale to this generation where a phone can just do that same function and you can immediately preview, select the ones you want, upload on the internet or print it without going through all those 'negative' stress. Lol!

DEALING WITH THE NEGATIVES

Now here's the lesson: Just like that old photography process, God makes men, not in the spotlight or in the conference of cheering fans, but at the backstage of insignificance. The entire fine picture you eventually see was made in the dark.

When God wants to set you up for destiny, He would have to flush out everything that contaminates your shine and usually at that point, what people would see is just your Negatives.

From the beginning it starts out with a flash, a sudden spotlight on you that just shows off your favourable qualities and commendable sides. At this point, everybody wants to identify with you based on the beauty they see. But in no time, the next version of you that hits the screen is your Negative, and all of a sudden your fan club turns critics because all they now see is the negatives.

At this point people would doubt your genuineness. You would lose your credibility and also platforms may shutdown on you. But the truth is, you're still in the process.

I'm tired of people that conclude on me because they saw my negative. Just hold on. Let me go back to the lab one more time. God is not done with me yet. I'm still in the process.

There is power in the negativity of your life, and God knows how to take your negatives into the darkness of where you can't see your way up or out, and turn it all into a positive beauty that cannot be ignored.

That shame is going to become success. That failure is turning into victory. That misery is going to become ministry. That indolence is going to become industry. That terrible terror in your life is going to become triumph.

If you understand this, then you'll appreciate that God deliberately puts you in the dark, not to hurt or destroy you, but to develop what He has called you for and why He gave you the gifts. And sometimes, we get into trouble because of what God gave us, but even at that, just know that the trouble was ordained by God for your ultimate profiting.

It hurts to know that most people never want to be part of the process, but they want to be part of the outcome. The process is where you figure out who's worth being part of the outcome. No matter how long it takes, hang in there. It may be slow, but quitting wont speed it up. If you quit now, you'll end up right back where you first began. Yeah! This is destiny working out in you. Stick to it!

The process is the most important part of the journey. I dare you to appreciate it while it lasts. "Trust the process. Your time is coming. Just do the work and the results will handle themselves." (Tony Gaskins)

I love the scripture in John 12:24 *"Most assuredly I say to you, unless a seed submits its potential to the soil and undergoes the process of insignificance, silence and despised, it never amounts to anything more; but if it dies, it eventually produces much harvest."* (Paraphrased)

I am careful about people that have always been significant. I am careful about people that have always been celebrated. I am careful about people that never go behind the curtain. I am careful about people that always carry the microphone. I am careful about people that are always the leaders. I am careful about people that always want to take control; always want to be at the front row, because in most cases, they have not undergone the process. So no matter how good they may seem right now, they have not undergone process.

These kinds of people break down under little pressure. They don't know what it means to be broke or to have a broken relationship, they have always been the super stars, always been the one that boys come after and when they are tired of this one they drop out, without having any heartbreak. They don't understand what it means to have losses in business.

Until you come to the point you are present but not recognized, you're still running on your startup energy. Have you noticed that before Jesus started his ministry, he was a member in John the Baptist's Church (*so to say*) and John the Baptist was preaching and called all of them vipers. Wait! Did he just call Jesus a viper? This is the Messiah, Lord of lords and the King of kings, for crying out loud. Yeah! But for 30 years he was in obscurity; without public notice. How long have you being behind the scene without public notice, without recognition and significance?

"For a seed to come into its own, it must become fully undone. The shell must break open, its inside must come out, and everything must change. If you didn't understand what life looks like, you might mistake it for complete destruction." (Ann Voskamp)

ACTIVITY SHEET

1. Recount past experiences where your 'negatives' surfaced in public view - where and when?
2. What did you lose as a result of that?
3. Do you ever feel a desire to make a comeback?

04: THE PROCESS OF REINVENTION_

"...unless a seed submits its potential to the soil and undergoes the process of insignificance, silence and despised, it never amounts to anything more; but if it dies, it eventually produces much harvest." (Paraphrased) -John 12:24

I'd like to carefully re-examine the words of Jesus in John 12:24 *"… unless a seed submits its potential to the soil and undergoes the process of insignificance, silence and despised, it never amounts to anything more; but if it dies, it eventually produces much harvest."* (*Paraphrased*) Oh wow!

The fact remains that there has always been life in that seed but that's not all about it. There's a forest inside that one seed, waiting for the due process to lunch into reality. God doesn't want the seed to just carry life, but to be a life giver.

So just like that seed, the process rips you of your initial status, you lose the message you have first... you lose your testimony... even mess-up yourself until there's almost nothing left in your record that qualifies you for honour, so that the excellency of the transformation and impact of your final outcome would not be of your ability or self-righteousness, but exclusively, God. At this time you know you're standing out, not by public endorsement based on a credible track record, but strictly by the grace of God.

How come you, a beautiful lady that your husband went on his knees to ask your hand in marriage, but now you can hardly sit him down to talk to him? Could it be that beyond facial beauty, there are other areas of your life that have to undergo some form of re-invention?

How come you that was best for the job initially, are now seeking for prayers and hands to be laid on you to retain that job? Could it be that you have not reinvented yourself? You were employed as a driver, but how much more can you now do, for which you should be retained, when the company undergoes downsizing? You have just being the best driver and now they don't need a driver anymore.

Have you ever considered running a short-term training on computer operation/maintenance, housekeeping, laundry, branding, multimedia, website design, hosting, or/and management, photography, safety course, firefighting ....during your annual leave or as a part-time program?

I'm talking about adding more value to yourself and the organization you find yourself, so you eventually have more value to offer than what you were employed for.

Until you come to this point, you have just been carrying life; you are not yet a life giver. "If you can't describe what you're doing as a process, you don't know what you're doing." (W. Edwards Deming)

Everybody or business you see thriving sustainably, has had times when they retreat to reinvent themselves, restructure and create new strategies on how to take over the market. Anything you have now without this kind of process is like that seed that never amounts to much. You must subject it to the process of planting, decomposing, germination and then fruiting.

Outside process potential is as cheap as a raw material. Process is the divine scheme for adding value to potential. Potential is God's responsibility; God put it in you. You didn't initiate it and you can't even improve on it. The most you can do is to develop capacity. Potential, is an implantation of God's intelligence. Where your work lies is to undergo the process.

Raw gold can be dug up from the rocks, but until it is refined, not many people appreciate its value. Crude oil could be found in the swamps where nobody want to have anything to do with, but when it is refined, people queue up in the petrol stations with their money to purchase it. You take on your true value by undergoing the due process.

It is the process that builds in you the capacity to handle the kind of pressures that knock others down. People that have always being right don't know what it feels like to face correction.

It takes process to be fully equipped and furnished to perform efficiently and effectively. Do the needful to improve your value.

Purpose is the drive, process is the route. The sense of Purpose helps you maximize the process.

ACTIVITY SHEET

1. What other skills would you like to develop?
2. When would you like to start?
3. How do you want this to improve your worth where you are now?

05: **TRAINED TO FUNCTION_**

"But in a great house there are not only vessels of gold and silver, but also of wood and clay, some for honour and some for dishonor. If therefore you keep yourself clean of these latter, you will be specially honourably useful, consecrated, fit for the Master's service, and fully equipped to (trained to function) for every good work." (Paraphrased) -2Tim. 2:20

CFO asks CEO: "What happens if we invest in developing our people and then they leave us?" CEO: "What if we don't, and they stay?"

A quote from Henry Ford, the founder of Ford motor company that inspires me so much is, "The only thing worse than training your employees and having them leave is not training them and having them stay."

If delivering your destiny mandate is of any importance to you, you will find a way to be trained. If it is not, you'll find an excuse not to train.

Training is not a periodic event. it is an ongoing process for self-discovery and competence development. I dare you to be stronger than your excuses.

2Tim. 2:20 says, ***"But in a great house there are not only vessels of gold and silver, but also of wood and clay, some for honour and some for dishonor. If therefore you keep yourself clean of these latter, you will be specially honourably useful, consecrated, fit for the Master's service, and fully equipped (trained to function) for every good work."*** (Paraphrased)

Process avails you the opportunity to be trained to function.

Heb. 13:21 further strikes on this, *"May God make you perfect in every good work, so that you may be able to do His will (fulfill His purpose for your life). May He bring out of you all He has deposited in you so that you may be pleasing in His sight..."* (Paraphrased)

Process is that system, put in place by God to bring out of you the good things He deposited in you, usually by training.

2Tim. 3:16-17 deepens it further, *"All scriptures are given by the inspiration of God, and is profitable for teaching, for correcting errors, for giving guidance, and for training others in righteousness, so that you may be complete, thoroughly equipped, trained and made ready for every good work."*

Isn't it amazing that even righteousness needs training, according this scripture?

My essence of taking you through all these scriptures is to emphasize that training is the essence of the process. Everything God is trying to achieve in the process is 'Training'.

Without training you are like a hazard about to happen. Without training you become a threat to any organization or even your relationship. It is by training you acquire the required experience for the job, assignment, ministry or even your relationship. It is by training you develop expertise, proficiency and skill. It then means that even the skill required for the job is not a divine impartation.

Whatever you had that got you the job initially was just your starter package. Now you have to reinvent yourself. Train again to improve your proficiency and increase your value.

SQUEEZE SOME MORE

Give an orange to a little child and watch him exhaust his strength in squeezing out the juice. You'd agree with me that at the end of his struggle, you can still squeeze some more juice out of that same orange. That means, there was so much more in the orange than the hard effort of the child could produce.

David stood before King Saul on the basis of his starter-pack anointing, which was just enough to get him in, but beyond the grace of acceptance, furthermore there was a grace of retention, and this is strictly a function of competence. Read **1Sam. 16:15-22.**

Your starter-pack gift may take you through the door and stand you before kings, but I bet it takes more than that to keep you much longer where value is constantly sort for. Competence is key *bae*.

Competence envisions and sustains you on the platform of value. Competence is the ability to be consistent in delivering value. Hence, the essence of training is to develop competence.

David had trained for years in obscurity, and when the opportunity came, he topped the chart; he came highly recommended. Please understand this: Job security is only entitled to people that have trained in obscurity.

Until you can standardize your productivity, you are not competent. Train more. Squeeze harder for more sweetness to come out of you. Yeah! It takes all that and some more.

IMPROVE OPPORTUNITIES

It is by training you develop expertise, proficiency and skill.
It is by training you learn the wisdom of buying time.

See what Eph. 5:15-16 says, ***"See then that you live and act wisely; not as fools but as wise, redeeming the time (improve opportunities, making the most of opportunities, buy opportunities, make time count) because the days are evil."***

Like I said earlier, you now have a job opportunity, God expects you to be wise enough to improve on that opportunity. Every opportunity you expend, after which you return to the very point you were before, reveals a measure of foolishness still resident in you, which can only be erased by training.

The wisdom of reinvention is to learn to capitalize on whatever you have or wherever you are right now, to create better opportunities for growth, expansion and exploits.

Training reduces and eventually subsides your limitations. I know of an illiterate driver of a multinational company who ended up being a contractor in that same company and an employer of labour himself. He started out as one of the least paid, but when this wisdom dawned on him, he realized he could offer more value and be commensurately rewarded more than he was earning. He took a risk of tasking his mind through a training process and he was amazed at his own creativity and ability to cross the limits of mediocrity into the realms of exceptional value.

The bitter truth is until you are trained you cannot even meet up to God's standard. *"You however, are to be trained to perfection, even as your Heavenly Father is perfect."* (Matt. 5:48 *paraphrased*). So even the perfection of the saints is a function of training.

This is why it is important you belong to a church and be committed; not as a floor member, but enroll as an active worker. Stop playing truancy with God. This is a serious deal.

Your making is in your training. Jesus said to his disciples *"...come follow me and I will make you..."* (Mark 1:17).

This was not a promise of a miracle like He did on other people they witnessed. This was a call to training by a set of Kingdom principles. Eventually, those men were the patriarchs to whom dispensations were committed to, with the gospel. Your assignment is bigger, so is your package.

Strength does not come from doing what you can do. It comes from overcoming the things you once thought you could not do. Whatever it takes, give it. Your outcome will be glorious.

ACTIVITY SHEET

1. What are the training options around you now?
2. What courses can you take now to add to your knowledge in respective areas of interest?
3. List out sites you can browse or people you can contact for vital information on this.

06: **PRODUCT_**

"And God blessed them, and God said unto them, Be fruitful, and multiply, and replenish the earth, and subdue it..." -Gen. 1:28

This is the third 'P' of Purpose.

Gen. 1:28 "And God blessed them, and God said unto them, Be fruitful, and multiply, and replenish the earth, and subdue it..."

This is a very regular scripture which has been so shallowed to the concept of mere procreation. This scripture has been so constrained in its depth and limited in its application to practical living.

From the earliest trace of human existence, God commanded:
"**...BE FRUITFUL ...**" *(in Hebrew <parah>)* this means to Cause impact... to produce tangible effect to the measure of your potential.
"**...MULTIPLY...**" *(in Hebrew <rabah>)* this means to make the most of ...to improve on something ...to increase geometrically.
"**...REPLENISH...**" *(in Hebrew <male'>)* this means to refill while in use.

I once saw an advert of an automobile company advertising one of their brands and the closing line was "...built for Nigerian roads." That struck me deep. The advert showed the truck bumping through gallops, insinuating, the manufacturers have taken into cognizance the reality of some bad roads in the country before building this particular truck to meet that specific need. Thereby, recommending their product to conquer the challenge of driving on bad roads.

PARAH

This is how God stocked you up with a lot of untapped abilities and crafted you in such a seamless posh view and released you into this world.

Every time you're faced with a tough situation, it is no time to chicken into a shell of insecurity, sense of inadequacy or fear of failure. That's your opportunity to cause a positive impact and produce a tangible effect. It's in you *bae*. Yeah! It's in you... the ability to change any situation and restore sanity, peace and order.
Everything happening around you right now calls for you to parah – cause a positive impact. The seed of greatness is in you. This is your season to be fruitful.

RABAH

One thing the process does it to prime you up for the right time and chance to make a bigger hit. In most cases, it is a culmination of small opportunities you give your best shot that accredits you with the endorsement needed for mega platforms. The better you become, the stronger your impact. Just like the ripples of waves on a water surface when a stone is dropped inside, so your impact spreads relative to the degree of your size per time.

The formula for impact is **(PxO =I)**; where P = preparation, O = opportunity, and I = impact.

So I dare you to rabah – multiply. Increase geometrically by taking up the challenge to fly your possible best as the opportunity presents itself. Make the most of this moment.

MALE□

You were created so dynamic that you can actually use one opportunity to create another. You were never meant to diminish on any resource God blesses you with.

I feel God placing a demand on you to male' – replenish, reload, stock-up again... don't run dry. Maintain your effect in an increasing order.

This is only possible when you stay connected to your Source and other resources divinely positioned at your disposal by providence.

It is not enough to be busy, but to be productive. Until your life is addressing a need, you're worth nothing. No matter how much of your potentials you have discovered, until it can answer to life's demands, you remain unknown.

The product therefore, becomes that potential or idea that has undergone process.

1Tim. 4:14 says, *"Do not neglect the gift that is in you… Meditate on these things (Be diligent in them. Occupy yourself with them, habitually practicing these duties); give yourself entirely to them (and be absorbed in them), that your progress (your growing proficiency and expertise in them, advancement and profit) may be evident to all."*

"Stop waiting for a producer. Produce yourself." (Marianne Williamson)

The 3P's of purpose in summary is all about discovering your potential, deploying the process by subjecting yourself to training, discipline and service, then delivering result (productivity).

ACTIVITY SHEET

1. In your assessment, how much (in monetary terms) do you worth for the value you offer?
2. What is your present wage? Determine the gap between what you worth and how much you are paid now.
3. To close up this gap, which other ideas or skills can you develop?

07: THE ORIGIN OF POTENTIAL_

"In the beginning God..." -Gen. 1:1

Have you ever asked to know where life began from? Have you ever wondered the earliest form of everything that ever existed in the past and presently? This childhood quest has inspired several different approaches in the bid to give an answer; ranging from mythical tales and mystical superstition by illiterate parents to evolution theories by scientific researchers.

Going through some documented research works by renowned scientists on the origin of life, the earth and nature generally, left me with more questions as to what was the intelligence behind the combination of the said elements that primarily composed the earliest form of natural life. Where did they come from? Why is that process not repeating itself again? Or why is it not repeatable by scientific means?

For crying out loud, the said elements that sparked up natural life are still very much present. Why is it not creating another earth somewhere else? Why are apes not still evolving into humans today? Come on! Ain't nobody thinking along with me?

Permit me to say it is foolishness not to acknowledge God as the Creator and Origin of all forms of life. *"The fool has said in his heart, 'There is no God'..."* Ps. 14:1.

Hmmmm! This level of foolishness is not the absence of the knowledge of the truth, but the denial of the truth. This generation of free thinkers is caught in this mess. Which fundamental organism of life has anyone been able to create without using anything else?

If you don't mind, I'd like to stick with the earliest documented, undoubtable and undisputable Word of God to examine the subject of beginnings, for it is written, *"In the beginning God…"* (Gen. 1:1).

God remains the only initiator of time, space and life. And we see the whole process involved in the formation, structure and design of natural life traceable to the intelligence of a superior being.

He set everything in motion and through the ages, grants humans access into the shallow waters of His infinite intelligence. The scripture records the sequence of God's creation in Genesis chapter One and Two.

It is interesting how God began by creating the primary source of every other creature and then activated their functions by His voice code. Follow me closely.

"Then God said, 'Let the earth bring forth grass, the herb that yields seeds, and the fruit tree that yields fruit according to its kind, whose seed is in itself, on the earth'" -Gen 1:11

"Then God said, 'Let us make man in our own image, according to our likeness, let them have dominion over the fish of the sea, over

the birds of the air, and over the cattle, over all the earth and over every creeping thing that creeps on the earth'" -Gen 1:26

"And the Lord God formed man from the dust of the ground ..." - Gen 2:7

Space would fail me to cascade the whole scriptures here. But do you observe something about these verses? God spoke to the source for everything he made. He spoke to the earth to bring forth the plants and beasts. He spoke to waters to bring forth fishes and other aquatic creatures. But when He wanted to create the human being, He didn't speak to the earth or animals, neither did He speak to the waters, but He spoke to Himself.

Could it be that God Himself is the raw material for making man? Emphatically, yes! Oh wow! God himself is the original raw material of the real man.

But how about Gen. 2:7? Doesn't that show we came from the dust of the ground? Nope! That was only an earth suit formed to contain the real you and enable you relate with and function in this terrestrial realm, express yourself and enjoy everything else God has stocked up in nature.

That scripture also shows that the physical formation of man was not an evolution of matter and chemical elements; God had to manipulate the soil in His intelligence to form an adaptable earth suit for man.

We come in different sizes, shapes and colours, but that doesn't in anyway measure superiority, genuineness or authenticity of quality. Our realness is in our originality – the real person God made first before constructing this earth suit.

May I preempt myself by saying here, never think you would have been better off in someone else's earth suit. You got what suits you. Flaunt it in confidence.

ACTIVITY SHEET

1. If you had an option, what other nationality, shape or size would you have preferred to have?
2. Why that preference?
3. If you were to meet God, what questions would you like to ask Him about you makeup?

08: THE SOURCE AND SUSTENANCE_

"He sustains all forms of life by the word of His creative power..." -
Heb. 1:3

We see a deeper dimension of the intelligence of God displayed in sustaining the life of everything made by allocating its habitat within its source. Outside the waters, the fish is limited in its life span. If you drop a lion in the midst of a sea, its primary interest would cease from preying on other animals to surviving, because that environment doesn't support its strength and bravery.

Outside your habitat, your entire intelligence is reduced to survival instincts. Maybe now you can understand why people 'hustle' just to survive daily.

Where people hustle is where there is no support system in place to provide necessary amenities for nourishment and growth.

My heart is so much pained with the increasing number of populace hustling just to survive on daily basis – infants and the aged hocking or begging on the streets, tricksters and gamblers, hoodlums and roadside thugs, ritual killers and cyber criminals, prostitutes and drug dealers, people doing all sought of jobs just to survive.

THE SOURCE CODE

Sadly, hustling has become such a household phenomenon, because the majority is ignorant of God's sustenance plan and procedure. Somebody once said, "Life would be much easier if I had the source code." Hmmm....! I'm handing you the 'source code' right here.

Sustenance is a system of support and nourishment. The sustenance of everything God created was conditioned on constant connection with its source. The plant has to stay in the soil to be nourished, grow and bear fruits. The fish has to remain in the water to live and reproduce. So also, you have to stay connected in God to live, thrive and maximize your full potential because you are an offspring of God (Ref.: **Ps. 82:6**).

"Abide in Me, and I in you. As the branch cannot bear fruit of itself, except it abides in the vine, neither can you, unless you abide in Me." (John 15:4)

"For it is in our closest union with Him that we discover true life, and are mobilized (animated and set in motion) in the right direction and secure our true identity (purpose for existence)….For we are His offspring" (Acts 17:28 paraphrased)

SOURCE DETERMINES BOUNDARIES

A deeper insight into this concept reveals that source determines boundaries. One active meaning of the word 'Plant' is to place something firmly in a particular spot or position. Don't you see how this rule, naturally followed, accounts for the vegetation around us? Just by sticking to the soil long enough, a little seed becomes a big tree and then, a forest of tress.

Could it be that you're stuck in your small seed form because you don't understand the discipline of restriction. You can't be in too many places all the time and still flourish. There is an allocated spot and condition supportive of your bloom. Outside that, you would struggle in your small seed form.

The desire for a wider reach is inherent in every potentially great tree, but this is not possible in a seed form. It has to be planted – constrained within a fixed space under certain conditions, and then the growth process begins till it branches out wide and reaches as far as it would, and also bears fruits endlessly.

If you want to make such an impact that would outlast you, I recommend you hookup with your Source. Only then can you be sure to break even with such an eternal relevance.

ACTIVITY SHEET

1. What would you have achieved at this point in your life, but for lack of proper support?
2. What support do you need now to be more stable?
3. What activities are you involved in now that makes you feel time-wasted, drains your passion and leaves you so exhausted?

09: POTENTIAL REVEALS IDENTITY_

"In the beginning God..." -Gen. 1:1

Identity is the features that distinguish one from another. It is your point of difference from others.

In other words, your identity is the odd thing about you amidst the similarities you may share with others. So trying to define yourself by the spectrum of social criteria is an underestimation of your individual uniqueness.

Your identity, in a nutshell, is your uniqueness – your distinctive difference. Your difference is your essence.

Dr. Mike Murdock said, "Wisdom is the recognition of difference." And that's so true. Alongside potential, the creation story also reveals difference – difference between the sun and the moon, difference between day and night, difference between land and sea, difference between humans and beasts, difference between man and woman... down to the difference between Cain and Able, and so on. Lol!

At some point Adam was going to be tested as God presented him with everything He had made, to name them. Literally, what God wanted was for him to identify everything by their difference. That was God run-testing his shared wisdom in Adam (Ref.: **Gen. 2:19-20**).

The harmony of life only gains appreciable wonder, when we consider how different elements complement themselves to form this beauty that we see.

Wherever there is more than one, if the individuals have to be identified, their difference must be considered. Difference is such a beautiful thing, it reveals distinctive identities. There is no identity in uniformity. Don't be afraid of being different, rather be afraid of being the same as everyone else. Enough of trying to be like anybody else. That is not what God made you. Be you!

One Huawei advert says, "Just be you. Everybody else is taken."

It doesn't make any sense regulating your behaviour to that of this world, but be changed and reset your mind, so that by experience you may explore the good and pleasing and complete purpose of God for your life. (Ref.: **Rom. 12:22** *BBE*).

::: Do not be configured, contaminated or infiltrated by the operating system of the world which influences you by environmental factors. Instead, constantly improve on your mind's capacity and enhance your mind productivity by replacing those outdated invalid way of life with the values of God's word. By this, you will progressively develop from the level of fundamental religious expectations to more commendable virtues until you close in on Gods specific purpose for your life.

Stop trying to conform to a system God has destined you to transform. Stop working in someone else's shadows, or become like a monster with several different faces of identity due to peoples different opinions of you which were drawn from your inconsistences at many different instances.

When would other people admire you for your difference?
In the school of destiny, there is no identity in uniformity.
Your difference is your essence.

Your identity is in your uniqueness, and your uniqueness is
an inexhaustible well of a lifetime research. Just when you
think you have seen enough of you, there is still more
untapped potential awaiting your discovery.

You share in one of the unique features of your Source –
God, which is omnipotence. You cannot be summarized by
generalization or public opinions.

You are not a sticky board, so stop letting every mess people
throw at you stick on your personality. I'm telling you today,
there is a whole lot in you now, than there is in your history.

IDENTITY, THE NEW FACE OF VALUE

A coach once told me, "People only patronize who they like,
know or trust." Where value is concerned, the identity of a
brand is what determines its patronage.

I bet there are more beautiful and longer lasting fashion accessories in Aba (the eastern part of my country) than those of Amani and Gucci. But these are already known and trusted brands that spell quality and elegance, so they have the market.

I bet there are more skillful footballers playing local football than the likes of Messi and Ronaldo, but they worth little or nothing on the global platform because they are not as much a brand.

Identity is the hallmark of value. Know who you are, believe in yourself and define yourself in the light of your potential.

The password to accessing your destiny is spelt IDENTITY.

The doors of destiny only respond to your right identity. You cannot impersonate your way into destiny. You cannot wear someone else's gift or looks and make it into your own destiny. Your destiny is customized to your own uniqueness. Be comfortable in your own skin. Be original.

The only authorized access into your destiny is authenticity. Accept yourself for who you are, or else you cannot get anybody else accepting you for who you are. You can't sell a product you don't believe in. Love yourself like you know there is something more in you that the world would soon be celebrating. Call it 'Self Crush' if you like.

You cannot tap into the resources of destiny without using your customized key, which is self-identity. When you don't have the keys, a door becomes a barrier.

Know who you are. Love who you are. Be original. "Originality consists of returning to the origin. Thus, originality means returning, through one's resources, to the simplicity of the early solutions." (Antonio Gaudi)

POTENTIAL IS REVEALED

The unearthing of your potential is the discovery of your true identity.

Identity is never defined in isolation. It can only be defined in relation to something.

Jesus spoke of the parable or tares among wheat in Matt. 13:24-30. Tares and wheat are lookalikes, but only one thing differentiates them, and that is their fruits – the manifestation of their individual potentials. Why one was called wheat and the other called tares can only be revealed in their final outcome.

Your true identity is a matter of revelation of your potential, not just observation of external traits or appearances.

Remember potential is not anything you've done; it is what you could do that you are yet to do. So identity is an ongoing unraveling of your personality based on your internal deposit. Don't you ever conclude on yourself based on past or present conditions. Keep tapping within.

Please understand the difference between 'identity' and 'description'. Too many times we end up describing ourselves in attempt to define ourselves. In the real sense, your true definition may not look like your present description.

This reminds me of Joseph the dreamer-boy in the Bible. He was still living off of everybody's benevolence as the kid bro of the house, yet by destiny, he was to sustain nations economically.

You will slow down your manifestation if you keep looking at the mirror to define yourself. The mirror only reflects, it doesn't define. Your definition is in your potential and your potential is in your Source. The tree has no bank of fruits it withdraws from, all it does is stay with its source (the earth) long enough till its fruiting season comes and there it goes manifesting its potential.

"For it is in our closest union with Him that we discover true life, and are mobilized (animated and set in motion) in the right direction and secure our true identity (purpose for existence)….For we are His offspring" (Acts 17:28 *paraphrased*).
You are lost in your primary search of true identity outside your source – God.

ACTIVITY SHEET

1. In your words, define yourself.
2. Identify your point of difference from people around you.
3. In the eyes of your deepest imagination, who do you see yourself becoming in the future?

10: THE EXCEPTIONAL RULE_

"Jesus answered and said unto him, Verily, verily, I say unto thee, Except a man be born again, he cannot see the kingdom of God." - John 3:3

The phrase 'Born Again' has come a long way. It is being seriously criticized for centuries, suffered so much social bias, constitutional disapproval, many attempts to be out-modeled by contemporary fashion and politically seen as an unpopular tool in legislation

Born Again in a simple term, is the process of making Jesus your Lord and personal Saviour by confessing His Lordship over your life and receiving forgiveness of sin and then you become the righteousness of God by faith.

This is about getting saved from the control and consequences of sin and thereby, qualifying through the blood sacrifice of Jesus Christ to enjoy the Kingdom life as a legal right. Being Born Again delivers you from death and destruction and re-establishes an eternal relationship with God.

Being Born Again is like the vaccination that cures the sin virus and its consequences. This is the reason why it is an 'EXCEPTIONAL RULE' and not an option.

"...for you have been born again not of seed which is perishable but imperishable, that is, through the living and enduring word of God." (1Pet.1:23)

"Therefore if anyone is in Christ, he is a new creature; old things are passed away; behold, all things have become new." (2Cor. 5:17)

Just as someone is first born into a physical family before being entitled to bear that family name and partake of their inheritance, so also you must first be born into God's family before bearing the name of God and qualifying to receive His family inheritance. Though God loves everyone, but not everyone is His child. The fact that a person knows that there is a God in heaven whom he fears or for the simple reason that someone is good behaved does not boycott this rule. You must be born into God's family.

Whoever fails to come to God through the only legitimate channel - Jesus, such a person may carry God's family name tag or hang around God's family members, have all the church stickers or branded clothes, that still does not make him or her a child of God. Such a person could better be termed as an imposter. Lol!

"Jesus said to him, "I am the way, the truth, and the life. No one comes to the Father except through Me." (John 14:6)

There are no substitutes or alternatives, you can only become a members of God's family by adoption through Christ Jesus. No one who by-passes Jesus ever gains approval into sonship!

Many good people are involved in some new age recommended accesses to God. However, the truth remains that those counsels cannot be justified with scriptures. There is only one means to God and that is salvation through Jesus Christ.

"...having predestined us to adoption as sons by Jesus Christ to Himself, according to the good pleasure of His will, to the praise of the glory of His grace, by which He has made us accepted in the Beloved. In Him we have redemption through His blood, the forgiveness of sin, according to the riches of His grace" (Eph. 1:5-7)

The process of salvation is supernatural and instantaneous. All you need do is believe in your heart and confess with your mouth the Lordship of Jesus over your life, and boom! That very moment, you are enlisted as a member of God's family and every wrong you have ever done in your entire life and its consequences are wiped away instantly.

"...For with the heart one believes unto righteousness, and with the mouth confession, is made unto salvation." (Rom. 10:10)

This is the God ordained prescription or initiation into the family of God. This process is called being Born Again. It is so simple and instant, yet the most powerful spiritual initiation of righteousness in the whole world.

This new relationship makes you His own and gives you His authority, equips you as an ambassador and puts you in position to start living a life of dominion in Christ.

When you get Born Again, Jesus gives you His inheritance, you become a seed of Abraham by faith, and the promises of God become accessible to you as He promised Abraham. The realization of such great promises in your physical life, becomes a product of the application of the principles of faith in God's Word.

God is not obligated to intervene in just any individual's life that has not submitted to Him. No father prioritizes feeding strangers on the streets using his resources. Jesus said, you cannot give what belongs to the children to dogs (Mark 7:27). This means that, it is the right of the children to receive God's promises as a matter of priority. One of such promises is healing for your body. The Bible says that healing is the children's bread.

A mistake many people make is thinking that after getting Born Again, their minds are instantly cleansed of all traces of ungodly thoughts. Don't assume that wrong desires and thoughts will just cease abruptly. When wrong thoughts pop up in your mind or you begin to feel same old way, don't panic or doubt the genuineness of your salvation. That could just be your mind feeding on what you see, hear or feel. And in other cases, it may just be revisiting the residue of your old nature. That doesn't mean you're not really Born Again; it only shows how much you need to renew your mind. Everybody that has ever made a decision for Christ faces these same issues and for most of us, we're still improving on our walk with God daily.

The fact is that, although the spirit man gets saved instantly, the mind requires a process of transformation to conform to God's image. This takes time, patience and effort to grow into maturity and then you begin to produce fruits of the new nature. This is called the fruit of the Spirit (Gal.5:22-23).

No tender plant produces tangible fruit in large quantity. Fruit bearing is a sign of maturity. When a seed is planted, it will shoot out, grow out a stem, produce branches, bring forth beautiful flowers and then begin to produce fruits according to the level of life within it (Matt. 13:25-34).

If you accept this Word into your heart as a seed, then the growth process begins right away until you start bearing fruits of righteousness. One thing is sure, trusting in the love of God for you, would always keep you desiring to please Him in your thoughts, actions and conduct.

The maximum wages sin offers is the worst type of death, which is separation from God and once you're cut off from your source you begin to hemorrhage to death (Rom.6:23). But when the law of the Spirit of life is introduced, everything begins to receive life. That which was dying will come alive again (Rom. 8:1-3). The Bible says, if the same Spirit that raised Jesus from death dwells in you, He shall quicken your mortal body; your health, marriage, business etc.

WHICH EVER WAY, YOU WIN

Someone once asked an interesting question, "Supposing a day comes when we all realize that there's no heaven or hell, and this 'Born Again' thing doesn't really count, won't it be regretful to know that we just forfeited so much 'fun' for nothing?"

Be honest with yourself, have you ever thought about this before? Well, I have, and this is what I think: Then I would have led a good and exemplary life; peaceful, honest, caring, a good citizen, been a role model to young people, kept a good commitment to healthy living, had a disciplined financial life and maintain good relationship with my neighbours. You see? Even without out-listing the spiritual benefits of being Born Again, it still would have been a good investment to have made with my life on earth. So whichever way, I win! It is not a loss for me.

I bet you, making this decision, you will never regret it. It might need some immediate sacrifice like cutting off from some certain things or pleasures, but the dividends are eternal. Accept Jesus now as your Lord and personal Saviour.

NOW SAY THIS PRAYER...

Dear Lord Jesus, I come to You today, I realize that I am a sinner and I'm lost without You. I need you in my life. I believe in my heart that You're the Son of God that came to die for my sins and resurrected for my justification. I confess with my mouth that You are the Lord of my life. Thank You for loving me so much. I declare, I am now Born Again. Amen!

If you just made that prayer, congratulations! You just started a glorious journey today. I'd like to hear from you and help answer any questions you might have. Kindly identify yourself by dropping me a message on any of our handles and my team and I will follow-up on you.

God bless you.